The World of Color

Blue in My World

by Joanne Winne

Children's Press
A Division of Grolier Publishing
New York / London / Hong Kong / Sydney
Danbury, Connecticut

Photo Credits: Cover and all photos by Thaddeus Harden
Contributing Editors: Mark Beyer and Magdalena Alagna
Book Design: Michael DeLisio

Visit Children's Press on the Internet at:
http://publishing.grolier.com

Library of Congress Cataloging-in-Publication Data

Winne, Joanne.
    Blue in my world / by Joanne Winne.
      p. cm. — (The world of color)
    Includes bibliographical references and index.
    Summary: A simple story highlights such blue things as blue jeans, blueberries, blue
sky, and blue water.
    ISBN 0-516-23123-5 (lib. bdg.) — ISBN 0-516-23048-4 (pbk.)
    1. Blue—Juvenile literature. [1. Blue. 2. Color.] I. Title.

QC495.5.W564 2000
535.6—dc21

                                                                                          00-024364

Contents

1   A Blue Bird   4

2   Blue with Breakfast   8

3   Blue at the Park   16

4   New Words   22

5   To Find Out More   23

6   Index   24

7   About the Author   24

My name is Matt.

This is my pet.

Do you know what this blue bird is called?

5

This bird is not a bluebird.

This bird is a **parakeet**.

Some parakeets are blue.

I am having breakfast.

I have **cereal** and **toast**.

Can you name the foods that are blue?

I have **blueberries** with my cereal.

Blueberry **jam** is on my toast.

I am going to the park.

I put on my **jacket** and hat.

Which clothes that I am wearing are blue?

12

13

I am wearing three blue things.

My jacket and hat are blue.

My **jeans** are blue, too.

15

I like to walk through the park.

I always visit the duck pond.

Can you guess what is blue at the park?

The sky is blue.

My toy boat is blue, too.

19

Blue can be found everywhere.

What do you see around you that is blue?

21

New Words

blueberries (**bloo**-ber-reez) a kind of
blue fruit

cereal (**seer**-ee-**ul**) a dry breakfast food
that you eat with milk

jacket (**jak**-it) a light coat

jam (**jam**) a sweet food that is spread on
bread or toast

jeans (**jeenz**) a kind of clothing

parakeet (**par**-uh-**keet**) a small bird

toast (**tohst**) bread that has been
cooked until it is brown

To Find Out More

Books
Beneath a Blue Umbrella
by Jack Prelutsky and Garth Williams
Greenwillow Books

Orchard's Little Blue Book of Nursery Rhymes
by Nila Aye
Orchard Books

Web Site
Crayola
www.crayola.com
This is the official Crayola Web site. It has a lot of
pictures to print and color, as well as craft ideas,
games, and online art.

Index

blueberries, 10

cereal, 8, 10

jacket, 12, 14
jam, 10
jeans, 14

parakeet, 6

toast, 8, 10

About the Author
Joanne Winne taught fourth grade for nine years, and currently writes and edits books for children. She lives in Hoboken, New Jersey.

Reading Consultants
Kris Flynn, Coordinator, Small School District Literacy, The San Diego County Office of Education

Shelly Forys, Certified Reading Recovery Specialist, W.J. Zahnow Elementary School, Waterloo, IL

Peggy McNamara, Professor, Bank Street College of Education, Reading and Literacy Program